The Race Across Alaska

by Carolyn Yee
illustrated by Dave Blanchette

Harcourt

Orlando Boston Dallas Chicago San Diego

Visit *The Learning Site!*
www.harcourtschool.com

The Iditarod is a race like no other. It is more than 1,000 miles long, and it is run across ice and snow. It takes at least nine days, and dogs are its stars.

The race got its name from the Iditarod Trail, an old mail road in Alaska. Long before there were telegraphs or phones, people used dogs to pull sleds that carried mail, supplies, and news. The sleds were driven by people called *mushers*.

The Iditarod race began in 1973. In the race, mushers use teams of twelve to sixteen dogs to pull sleds. The sleds are very light, and the mushers do not carry anything that they may not need. The lighter the sled, the faster the dogs can go.

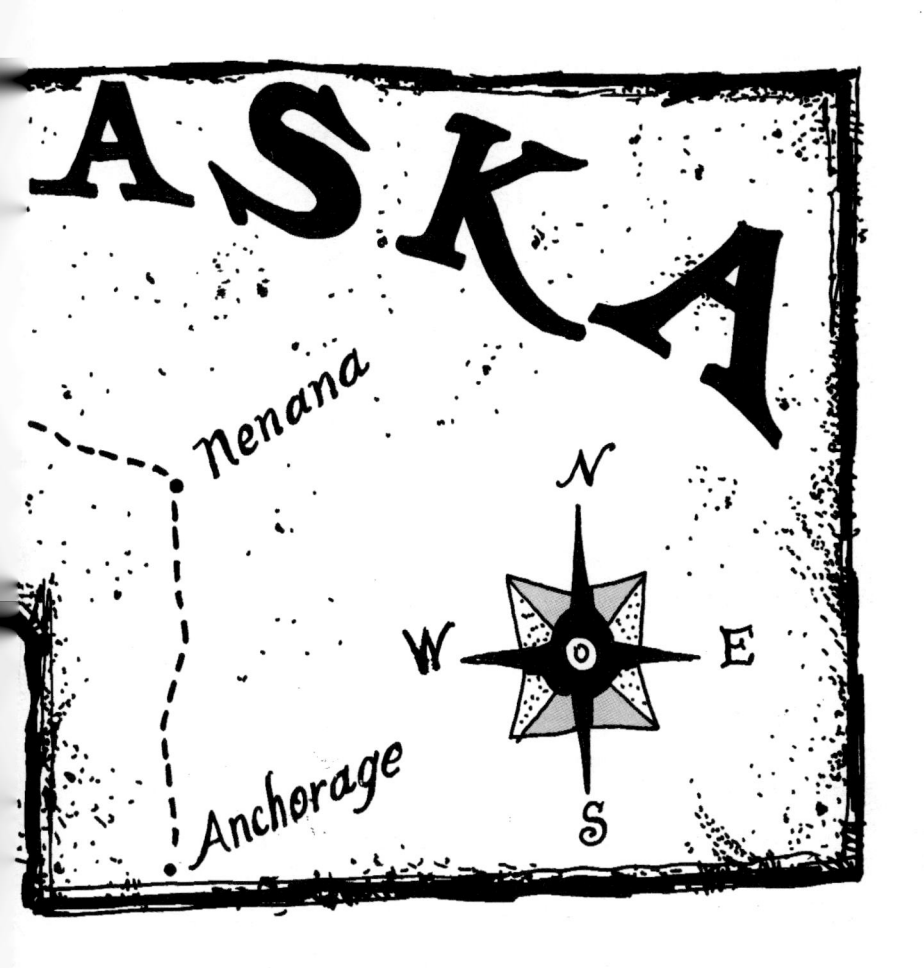

The Iditarod Trail runs from Anchorage to Nome, Alaska. It goes through cities and towns. The dog teams climb mountains. They race on frozen rivers. They run through deep drifts of snow.

The temperature may be far below zero, and the weather may be bad. Mushers have guided their dogs through howling ice storms, in which splinters of ice whirl through the air.

The dogs that run this race are amazing. They are very strong. One dog can pull nearly 1,000 pounds. They are also fast. The dogs can run from eight to twelve miles in one hour.

Mushers take good care of their dogs. They make sure that the dogs get plenty of food. They put booties on the dogs to keep splinters of ice from cutting their paws.

In 1998, sixty-three teams came from all over the world to be in the race. One of the mushers was named Jeff King. He had won the Iditarod twice before. DeeDee Jonrowe was racing again, too. She was known as a very good musher.

The weather during the 1998 Iditarod was so warm that the teams slept during the day and raced at night. The colder temperatures at night allowed the wet snow to freeze solid. Then the teams had hard trails to run on.

The 1998 Iditarod started out as a very fast race. Fifty of the teams were within twelve hours of each other. DeeDee Jonrowe was in the lead. She had been in the race sixteen times and had finished second twice. Jonrowe really wanted to win.

DeeDee's team was the first to reach the icy coast. The other teams were falling back, but Jeff King's team was close behind hers. Hour after hour, King came closer.

As they raced along the sea ice, Jonrowe's sled smashed against an icy drift. When she stopped to fix it, Jeff King sped ahead. Jonrowe worked quickly. Soon she was off again. The winds were stronger now. The record pace began to slow.

About twelve hours from Nome, a storm struck. Jeff King began to wonder if he really wanted to try any more. His dogs didn't give up, though. Red was his lead dog. Red was the best lead dog King had ever had.

The temperature kept dropping. It was the worst weather King had seen in six Iditarod races. The wind blew so hard the snow hit the racers sideways. The last part of the race, which should have taken two hours, took four.

After nine days, five hours, and fifty-two minutes, Jeff King crossed the finish line in Nome. DeeDee Jonrowe came in second three hours behind him. King had won the race in the third-fastest time ever. Now it was time for the racers and their dogs to rest.